WIGGLESWORTH on PRAYER

A 30-DAY DEVOTIONAL

Edited and Compiled by
Larry Keefauver

CREATION HOUSE

Creation House
Strang Communications Company
600 Rinehart Road
Lake Mary, FL 32746
Phone: 407-333-3132
Fax: 407-333-7100
Web site: http://www.creationhouse.com

All Scripture quotations are from
the King James Version of the Bible.

First printing, July 1996
Second printing, October 1996
Third printing, March 1997

A word about the cover:
The writing in the background is the actual
handwritten letter that Smith Wigglesworth
started the day before he died. His letter
shares the details of the healing of a woman
from cancer through his ministry.

Introduction

elcome to this thirty-day journey of faith with Smith Wigglesworth. What is so intriguing about this uneducated English plumber? As I began my research, I found myself mesmerized by the original sermon notes, Bible studies and pamphlets of Smith Wigglesworth. Delightful nuggets of spiritual truths filled those brown, aging pages from the past.

This devotional series shares some of the original Smith Wigglesworth with you. I pray that your relationship with the Lord, your walk in the Spirit and your intimacy with the Father will deepen as you read afresh the words God gave a humble plumber who brought revival to his generation.

We have kept our editing of Wigglesworth to a minimum. While his language may be unpolished at times, the force and power of his expression will speak to your life.

Called a "twentieth-century apostle," Wigglesworth became a legend as God mightily used him in an evangelistic and healing ministry. Born in 1859 in Menston, Yorkshire, England, he was converted in a Wesleyan Methodist meeting at age eight and pursued a career in plumbing. He married Polly Featherstone, and he and Polly operated a little mission in Bradford, England.

In 1907, Smith Wigglesworth received the baptism of the Holy Spirit, which radically changed him and transformed his ministry into a worldwide phenomenon. Literally thousands were saved and untold scores were healed by God's power as Wigglesworth preached powerful messages throughout the world. He went home to the Lord he loved in 1947.

Smith Wigglesworth often mentioned that he never read any other book than the Bible. For Wigglesworth, the Scripture was alive and embodied with the living Word of Christ. Likewise, the believer incarnated the Word in his daily walk. Prayer was an act of faith that claimed the truth of God's Word as a sure foundation for victory in all of life's trials. Discover Wigglesworth's timeless insights into God's Word and prayer as you use this devotional.

As you read this booklet, take time daily in God's Word. Each devotional contains a scripture, a principle about prayer from Smith Wigglesworth and a prayer to commit that meditation to reality in your life. Receive power and inspiration for your daily walk with the Lord!

I give all honor and praise to God the Father and Jesus Christ the Son for sending the Holy Spirit to inspire servants like Smith Wigglesworth to share such glorious truth and revelation so that mine and future generations might be truly blessed in Him!

Larry Keefauver, editor
1996

Praying and God's Word

He [God] sent his word, and healed them, and delivered them from their destructions.
Psalm 107:20

Are you ready? What for? That you may move and be moved by the mighty power of God that cannot be moved, and so chastened and built up till you are in the place where it doesn't matter where the wind blows or what difficulties arise. You are fixed on God.

Are you ready? What for? To come into the plan of the Most High God, believing what the Scripture says and holding fast to that which is good, believing no man shall take your crown.

God can so change us by His Word that we are altogether different day by day. David knew this. He said, "thy word hath quickened me" (Ps. 119:50). "He sent his word, and healed them" (Ps. 107:20). How beautiful it is that God makes His word abound! I have hid thy word in my heart that I might not sin against Thee.

It is absolute infidelity and unbelief to pray about anything in the Word of God.

Prayer Principle #1

__The Word of God does not need to be prayed about: The Word of God has to be received.__

If you will receive the Word of God, you will always be in a big place. If you pray about the Word of God, the devil will be behind the whole thing. Never pray about anything which is "Thus saith the Lord." It has to be yours to build you on a new foundation of truth.

Pray this closing prayer today:

Lord, grant me the strength and boldness to stand firm on Your Word, receiving Thy Word for all my needs. Amen.

EXCERPTED: "Workers Together With God," Bible study no. 15, 28 July 1927, 2.

Praying Anywhere and Everywhere

*Praying always with all prayer and
supplication in the Spirit.*
Ephesians 6:18

When traveling by ship from England to Australia, these people came round me and said, "We want to know if you will join us in an entertainment." So I had to go quietly to the Lord and ask, "Can I?" I had the sweetest rest about it being all right.

So I said, "Yes, I will be in the entertainment." They said, "What can you do?" "I can sing," I said. Then they said to me, "Well, we have a very large program and would like to put you down to sing a song." "Oh," I said, "my song will be given just before I sing. So you cannot put it down until I am to sing."

They said, "We are very anxious to know what place you would like to be put in the entertainment." "Well, how are you going to finish up?" I asked. "We're going to finish with a dance," they replied. "Put me down just before the dance," I said.

My turn came. A woman, half-dressed, no sleeves, no skirts, came to play for me. I gave her the music. "Oh," she said, "I never, never could play that kind of music." "Don't you be troubled now," I said. "I have music and words." I sang:

> *If I could only tell it as I know it,*
> *My Redeemer who has done so much for me;*
> *If I could only tell you how much He loves you,*
> *I am sure that you would make Him yours today.*
> *Could I tell it? Could I tell it?*

I never could tell it. The people were weeping all over. The dance was put off. They couldn't have a dance. But we had lots of prayer meetings. We had some fine young men give themselves to Jesus.

Prayer Principle #2

Pray anywhere and everywhere.

Pray this closing prayer today:

> *Father God, grant me the boldness to transform any place I am into an occasion for prayer. Amen.*

EXCERPTED: "Sons of God," Bible study no. 7, 14 July 1927, 11-12.

Believe the Word of God

Verily, verily I say unto you, He that believeth on me hath everlasting life. I am that bread of life.
John 6:47-48

I tell you there is a redemption, there is an atonement in Christ, a personality of Christ to dwell in you. There is a godlikeness for you to attain unto, a blessed resemblance of Christ, of "God in you" that shall not fail if you believe the Word of God.

Prayer Principle #3

The living Word is sufficient for thee. Eat it. Devour it. It is the Word of God.

Were you ever able to fathom the fullness of that redemption plan that came to you through believing in Jesus? In the first place, He was "of God." He was called "The Word." He became flesh! Then, He was filled with the Holy Ghost. Then, He became the "operation" or "voice."

Jesus was the operation of the Word, by the power of God through the Holy Ghost and so He became "the Authority."

You are born of an incorruptible power of God, born of the Word, who has the personality, the nature of God. You were begotten of God, and you are not your own. You are now incarnated, so you can believe that you have passed from death unto life and have become an heir of God and a joint heir of Christ in the measure in which you believe His Word.

Pray this closing prayer today:

Thank you, Jesus, for birthing Thy Word in me that I might live by and feed upon Thy Word continually. Amen.

EXCERPTED: "The Incarnation of Man," (North Melbourne, Australia: Victory Press, n.d.) reprinted from the pamphlet "Good News," 4.

The Piercing Sword of God's Word

For the word of God is quick, and powerful, and sharper than any twoedged sword, piercing even to the dividing asunder of soul and spirit, and of the joints and marrow, and is a discerner of the thoughts and intents of the heart.

Hebrews 4:12

The Word, the life, the Presence, the power in your body, in the very marrow of your bones must be discharged throughout your whole being. The Word, the Life, the Christ which is the Word, separates in you soul from spirit — what a wonderful work! The Spirit divides you from soul affection, from human weakness, from all depravity, from the human soul in the blood of man. The blood of Jesus can cleanse your blood till the very soul of you is purified and your very nature is destroyed by the nature of the living Christ.

I speak to you precisely on resurrection touches.

Prayer Principle #4

We have come into divine resurrection touches in Christ.

The greatest work God ever did on the face of the earth was done in the operation of His power. Jesus was raised from the dead by the operation of God's mighty power. The operation in our hearts of that same resurrection power will dethrone self and will build God's temple.

Callousness will have to change. Hardness will have to disappear. All evil thoughts must be gone. Raised up will be lowliness of mind. This is a wonderful plan for us. How will it come to pass? His Word transforming, resurrecting, giving thoughts of holiness, inspiring intense zeal and giving us a desire for all of God till we live and move in the atmosphere of holiness.

Pray this closing prayer today:

Word of God, pierce my heart and touch my whole being with Thy resurrection power. Amen.

EXCERPTED: "Ephesians 4:1-16," Bible study no. 9, 3-4.

Prayer Changes Hearts

*The Pharisee stood and prayed thus
with himself, God, I thank thee,
that I am not as other men are,
extortioners, unjust, adulterers, or
even as this publican. I fast twice in
the week, I give tithes of all that I
possess. And the publican, standing
afar off, would not lift up so much
as his eyes unto heaven, but smote
upon his breast, saying, God be
merciful to me a sinner. I tell you,
this man went down to his house
justified rather than the other: for
every one that exalteth himself shall
be abased; and he that humbleth
himself shall be exalted.*
Luke 18:11-14

I know this as clearly as anything, that no man can change God. You cannot change Him.

There is a word in Finney's lectures which is very good. "Can a man who is full of sin and all kinds of ruin in his life, change God when he comes out to pray?" No, it is impossible.

But as a man labors in prayer, and groans, and travails because his tremendous sin is weighing him down, he becomes broken in the presence of God. When properly melted in the perfect harmony with the divine plan of God, then God can work in that clay where before He could not work.

Prayer Principle #5

Prayer changes hearts but it never changes God.

God is the same today and forever, full of love, of entreaty, of helpfulness.

Pray this closing prayer today:

*Heavenly Father, change me
as I pray. Amen.*

EXCERPTED: "Faith (Part Two)," message presented at Glad Tidings Tabernacle, 3 August 1922, 2.

You Are an Epistle of God's Word

Forasmuch as ye are manifestly declared to be the epistle of Christ ministered by us, written not with ink, but with the Spirit of the living God; not in tables of stone, but in fleshy tables of the heart.

2 Corinthians 3:3

It is true that we must be the epistle of Christ. The epistle of Christ is a living power in the mortal flesh, quickening, dividing asunder everything which is not of the Spirit, till you realize that now you live in a new order. It is the Spirit that has manifested Himself in your mortal body, the Word has become life.

Prayer Principle #6

The Word has quickened you all through and you are not in any

***way subject to anything around
you. You are above everything.
You reign with Christ above
everything.***

For you to live is to be His epistle, emblem-
atic, divinely sustained by another power
greater than you. So you do not seek your
own anymore. You are living in a place where
God is on the throne. He reigns in your
human life. God is changing you and making
you understand this wonderful truth — you
are Christ's epistle!

Pray this closing prayer today:

*Christ, make of my life Thy epistle to the
world. Write Thy salvation, Thy holiness,
Thy redemption, Thy good news on my
heart that others may read in me
only of Thee. Amen.*

EXCERPTED: "2 Corinthians 3," Bible study no. 16, 29 July 1927, 2.

Bethel—The Place of Prayer

And Jacob awaked out of his sleep, and he said, Surely the Lord is in this place; and I knew it not. And he was afraid, and said, How dreadful is this place! This is none other but the house of God, and this is the gate of heaven...And he called the name of that place Bethel.

Genesis 28:16-17,19

Is He your God? He is the God of the sinner. Oh, there is something wonderful about it. He is the God of the helpless. He is full of mercy. I tell you He is your God, and He is prepared to meet you exactly as He met Jacob.

For Jacob had deceived in every way. He had deceived to get his birthright; to get his cattle. He was a deceiver. Truly, the devil had a big play with Jacob, but, praise God, there was one thing that Jacob knew. Jacob knew that God fulfilled His promises. There in Bethel, God let him see the ladder, and it was a wonderful ladder, for it reached from earth to heaven. He saw angels ascending and descending. I am glad that the angels began at the bottom and came to the top. It was a lovely ladder, I tell you, if they could begin at the bottom and go to the top.

Prayer Principle #7

Just like Jacob in prayer, we begin at the bottom and go to the top.

Bethel — the place of prayer; the place of changing conditions; the place where we start on earth and enter heaven.

Pray this closing prayer today:

Father, I come to Bethel, Thy house of prayer, to start on earth and to climb into the heavenlies for I long to be with Thee. Amen.

EXCERPTED: "The Abiding Spirit," address presented in Adelaide, Australia, n.d., 6.

The Word in Your Heart

Thy word have I hidden in mine heart,
that I might not sin against thee.
Psalm 119:11

Thy word is a lamp unto my feet,
and a light unto my path.
Psalm 119:105

I would like the day to come that we would never come to a meeting without having the Word of God with us. The great need today is more of the Word. There is no foundation apart from the Word.

Prayer Principle #8

The Word not only gives you foundation, but it puts you in a place where you can stand, and

**after the battle keep on standing.
Nothing else will do that.**

When the Word is in your heart, it will preserve you from the desire to sin. The Word is the living presence of that divine power that overcomes the world. You need the Word of God in your hearts that you might be able to overcome the world.

Pray this closing prayer today:

*Lord, I will meditate on Thy Word
Prepare my heart that I might hide
Thy Word therein and be so
strengthened that I may have no
desire of sin in me. Amen.*

EXCERPTED: "Testing of Spirits," Bible study no. 10, 20 July 1927, 1.

Believe the Word of God

*And they overcame him [the devil]
by the blood of the Lamb, and by the
word of their testimony; and they
loved not their lives unto the death.*
Revelation 12:11

ave we been with Jesus? Do not think you will comfort people by singing wonderful hymns — they are lovely. Do not think you will comfort people any other way but by the Word of God being manifest because you have been with Jesus. There must be the law of the Spirit of life in Christ Jesus that shall put to death every other thing but His Word.

Prayer Principle #9

It is one thing to read the Word of God. It is another thing to believe it.

It is possible to be real and earnest and have zeal and fastings, and yet not to have faith. Do you not know that one little bit of faith which can only come through the Word of God is worth more than all your cryings, all your rolling on the floor, and all your screaming. God is better than all of this.

May the Holy Ghost give us today an inward knowledge of what it is to believe the Word of God. It is God's purpose to make every believer able to subdue everything and to be whole, perfect and an overcomer in Christ.

Pray this closing prayer today:

Word of God, richly indwell me that I might have an overcoming faith to subdue all worldly things in my life. Amen.

EXCERPTED: A teaching on John 7:37-39, n.d., 6.

Praying in Prison

Giving no offence in anything, that the ministry be not blamed; But in all things approving ourselves as the ministers of God, in much patience, in afflictions, in necessities, in distresses, in stripes, in imprisonments, in tumults, in labours, in watchings, in fastings.
2 Corinthians 6:3-5

In Switzerland I have been put in prison twice for this wonderful work. But, praise God, I was brought out all right!

The officers said to me, "We find no fault. We are so pleased. We have found no fault because you are such a great blessing to us in Switzerland."

And in the middle of the night they said, "You can go."

I said, "No, I will only go on one condition. That is that every officer there is in this place gets down on his knees and I pray with all of you."

Glory to God!

Pray this closing prayer today:

Lord, in the midst of my prisons, give me the wisdom to pray and not to moan and groan. Amen.

EXCERPTED: "Workers Together With God," Bible study no. 15, 28 July 1927, 15.

The Word and the Kingdom

*Let the word of Christ dwell in you
richly in all wisdom; teaching and
admonishing one another in psalms
and hymns and spiritual songs,
singing with grace in your hearts
to the Lord.*

Colossians 3:16

I believe that God wants to bring to our eyes and our ears a living realization of what the Word of God is, what the Lord God means, and what we may expect if we believe it. I am certain that the Lord wishes to put before us a living fact which shall by faith bring into action a principle which is within our own hearts, so that Christ can dethrone every power of Satan.

Come, this is my point.

The kingdom of heaven is within us, within every believer. The kingdom of heaven is the Christ, is the Word of God.

The kingdom of heaven is to outstrip everything else, even your own lives. It has to be so manifested that you have to realize even the death of Christ brings forth the life of Christ.

The kingdom of heaven is the life of Jesus, it is the power of the Highest. The kingdom of heaven is pure; it is holy. It has no disease, no imperfection.

Pray this closing prayer today:

Word of God, stir up richly within me that the kingdom of heaven might be manifested. Amen.

EXCERPTED: "Christ in Us," pamphlet (North Melbourne, Australia: Victory Press, n.d.), 6.

Praying as the Spirit Prays

*Likewise the Spirit also helpeth our
infirmities: for we know not what
we should pray for as we ought: but
the Spirit itself maketh intercession
for us with groanings which cannot
be uttered.*

Romans 8:26

We must have life in everything. Who knows how to pray but as the Spirit prayeth? What kind of prayer does the Spirit pray? The Spirit always brings to your remembrance the mind of the Scriptures and brings forth all your cry and your need better than your words. The Spirit always takes the Word of God and brings your heart, and mind, and soul, and cry, and need into the presence of God.

So we are able to pray only as the Spirit prays, and the Spirit only prays according to the will of God, and the will of God is all in the Word of God. No man is able to speak according to the mind of God and bring forth the deep things of God out of his own mind.

Prayer Principle #12

When we have entered in with God into the mind of the Spirit, we will find that God ravishes our hearts.

Now I can see that the Holy Ghost so graciously, so extravagantly puts everything to one side that He may ravish our hearts with a great inward cry after Jesus. The Holy Spirit "lusteth to envy" for you to have all the divine will of God in Christ Jesus in your hearts.

Pray this closing prayer today:

Holy Spirit, ravish my heart. Set aside all detractions from Thee. Pray through me that my heart's cry might be heard in the presence of God. Amen.

EXCERPTED: "Ye Are Our Epistle," message presented at Glad Tidings Tabernacle, 23 August 1922, 2.

The Word, Not Feelings

*For this cause also that we thank God
without ceasing, because, when ye
received the word of God which ye
heard of us, ye received it not as the word
of men, but as it is in truth, the word
of God, which effectually worketh also
in you that believe.*

1 Thessalonians 2:13

Oh, that God shall give us an earnest, intent position where flesh and blood have to yield! We will go forward. We will not be moved by our feelings.

The man who is prayed for tonight and gets a blessing, but tomorrow, because he does not feel exactly as he thinks he ought to feel, begins murmuring. So, he exchanges the Word of God for his feelings.

What an awful disgrace it is for you to change the Word of God because of your feelings.

Let Christ have His perfect work. You must cease to be. That is a difficult thing for you and me. But it is not trouble at all when you are in the hands of the Potter. You are only wrong when you are kicking. You are all right when you are still and He is forming you afresh.

So let Him form you afresh today and make of you a vessel that will stand the stress.

Pray this closing prayer today:

Word of God, take priority over my feelings that I must trust only Thy truth. Amen.

Excerpted: "Temptation Endured," Bible study no. 12, 22 July 1927, 5,7.

God's Truth in Our Hearts

But the word is very nigh unto thee,
in thy mouth, and in thy heart, that
thou mayest do it...In that I command
thee this day to love the Lord thy
God, to walk in his ways, and to
keep his commandments and his
statutes and his judgments, that
thou mayest live and multiply: and
the Lord thy God shall bless thee
in the land whither thou goest
to possess it.
Deuteronomy 30:14,16

I believe that God wants to bring our eyes and our ears to a living realization of what the Word of God is, what the Lord God means, and what we may expect if we believe it.

I am certain that the Lord wishes to put before us a living fact which shall by faith, bring into action a principle which is within our own hearts, so that Christ can dethrone every power of Satan.

Prayer Principle #14

It is only the truth of God's Word revealed to our hearts that can make us so much greater than any idea of ourselves that we had.

I believe that there are volumes of truth right in the midst of our own hearts. There is the need for revelations and for stirring ourselves up to understand the mightiness which God has within us. We may prove what He has accomplished in us if we will only be willing to accomplish that which He has accomplished in us.

Pray this closing prayer today:

Lord, reveal Thy Word in my heart that I might know Thy mighty power in my life. Amen.

EXCERPTED: "Christ in Us," pamphlet (North Melbourne, Australia: Victory Press, n.d.), 1-2.

Loving God's Word

*How sweet are thy words unto my
taste! yea, sweeter than honey
to my mouth.*
Psalm 119:103

One thing God has given to me from my youth up, and I am so thankful, is a taste or relish for no other book except the Bible. I can say before God, I have never read a book but the Bible, so I know nothing about books.

As I have peeped into books, I have seen in some of them perhaps one reason for good people to say, "That is a good book." Oh, but how much better to get the Book of books which contains nothing but God. If a book is commended because it has something about God in it, how much more shall the Word of God be food for the soul, the strengthening of the believer, and the building up of the human order of character with God, so that all the time he is being changed by the Spirit of the Lord from one state of glory into another.

We shall become flat, anemic and helpless without the Word, dormant and so helpless to take hold of the things of God.

Prayer Principle #15

You are not any good for anything apart from the Word.

The Word is everything. The Word has to become everything. When the heavens and the earth are melted away, then we shall be as bright, brighter than the day, and going on to be consistent because of the Word of God.

Pray this closing prayer today:

I love Thy Word, Oh God. It is sweet to my taste and life to my being Thy Word I cherish with my whole heart. Amen.

EXCERPTED: "Faith (Part Two)," message presented at Glad Tidings Tabernacle, 3 August 1922, 5.

The Word Imparts Life

It is the spirit that quickeneth; the flesh profiteth nothing: the words that speak unto you, they are spirit, and they are life.

John 6:63

One thing that the saints need to get to know is not how to quote Scripture but how the Scripture should be pressed out by the Spirit that the Spirit should impart life as the Word is given. Jesus says, "My word is the spirit of life."

Prayer Principle #16

So, we need the Spirit to bring life into the believer, imparting life through the Word.

Imparting life? Why? How? There is a deep

secret right in the midst of this, "[he] that hath this hope in him [Jesus] purifieth himself" (1 John 3:3).

There is a lovely word along this line in the eleventh chapter of 1 Corinthians, "For if we would judge ourselves, we should not be judged. But when we are judged, we are chastened of the Lord, that we should not be condemned with the world" (vv. 31-32).

Pray this closing prayer today:

Word of God, press in on my heart
that the Spirit might press it out of me
in Jesus' name. May I not simply quote
Scripture to those I meet everyday, but may I
rather impart the life of Christ to those who
need Him. Amen.

Excerpted: "Sons of God," Bible study no. 7, 14 July 1927, 8-9.

Sanctified By Thy Word

*Sanctify them through thy truth:
thy word is truth.*

John 17:17

Thy Word is truth. Sanctify them through Thy Word, which is truth. No child of God ever asks a question about the Word of God. What do I mean? The Word of God is clear on breaking bread, on water baptism and on so many things. No person who is going on to obedience and sanctification of the Spirit will pray over the Word.

Prayer Principle #17

The Word of God is to be swallowed, to be obeyed, not to pray over.

If you ever pray over the Word of God there

is some disobedience. You are not willing to obey. If you come into obedience of the Word of God, then when it says anything about water baptism, you will obey. When the Word speaks about tongues you will obey what it says about speaking in tongues. When the Word says anything about breaking bread and assembling yourselves together, you will obey.

When you are sanctified by the Spirit, you will be obedient to everything revealed in God's Word. In the measure you are not obedient, you will not come into the sanctification of the Spirit.

Pray this closing prayer today:

Holy Spirit, sanctify me by Thy truth and Word, that I might obey Thy Word without reservation. Amen.

EXCERPTED: "Rising Into the Heavenlies," address presented in Wellington, New Zealand, 24 January 1924, 3-4.

Take the
Word of God

As for God, his way is perfect:
the word of the Lord is tried:
he is a buckler to all those
that trust in Him.

Psalm 18:30

So I pray that you will think seriously in your heart about this: You have to be in the world, but not of it. Be a personal manifestation of the living Christ. Just as Christ was walking about the earth, you have to walk about as a son of God, with power and manifestation, because the people have not time to read the Bible, so you have to be the walking epistle, "read and known of all men."

You have to see rightly that Jesus is the Word. You have to believe the Word of God, not changing it because people have other opinions.

Prayer Principle #18

Take the Word of God. It will furnish you in every good stand.

In taking God's Word, you will discover that you want nothing better because there is nothing better. It is in His Word that you will find all you want — food when you hunger; light in your darkness; largeness of heart and thoughts inspired by God.

Pray this closing prayer today:

Lord, Thy Word will stand no matter what man says. Thy Word satisfies my every need. It is sustenance for my spirit; it guides my feet aright and inspires my mind to Godliness. Amen.

EXCERPTED: "God Bless You!" Bible study no. 4, 8 July 1927, 4.

Believing, Obeying and Prospering in the Word

This book of the law shall not depart out of thy mouth; but thou shalt meditate therein day and night, that thou mayest observe to do according to all that is written therein: for then thou shalt make thy way prosperous, and then thou shalt have good success

Joshua 1:8

God wants strong people. Remember the charge God gave Joshua when he said, "Be strong and of a good courage...neither be thou dismayed" (Josh. 1:9). And then He gave him the charge. If God forecasts anything for you, He will give you the power to carry it through.

So, after He had given Joshua the Word, He said, "Now it will depend upon your living, day and night meditating on the Word of God."

As you come into this blessed state of reverence for the Word of God, it will build you up also and make you strong.

"Then thou shalt have good success." He told Joshua that, in this state of grace, whenever he put his foot down, not to let it slide back, but to put the other foot ready for going forward. The devil brings back to peoples' minds those things which they did so long ago, and there they are, thinking about them day and night.

There are some things for certain. First, you will never forget your sins. Second, God has forgotten them. Third, the devil will try to make you remember your sins. The question is, are we going to believe God, the devil or ourselves? God says our sins are passed, cleansed, *gone!* You cannot go on with God till you stand on His Word as "cleansed," with the heart made pure.

Pray this closing prayer today:

Jesus, I believe Thy Word, not mine or the devil's. I am cleansed from all my sin by Thy blood. Hallelujah! Amen.

EXCERPTED: "Ordination," address given in Adelaide, Australia, n.d., 1.

The Word in You

I am crucified with Christ: nevertheless I live; yet not I, but Christ liveth in me: and the life which I now live in the flesh, I live by the faith of the Son of God, who loved me, and gave himself for me.

Galatians 2:20

The sons of God are being manifested. Glory is now being seen. The Word of God is becoming so expressed in the life of a son of God that natural life is ceasing and the Word begins to live fully in him.

How can Christ live in you? There is no way for Christ to live in you but only by the manifested Word in you, through you, manifestly declaring every day that you are a living epistle of the Word of God.

Beloved, God would have us to see that no man is perfected or equipped on any lines except as the living Word abides in him.

It is the living Christ; it is the divine likeness of God; it is the express image of Him; and the Word is the only factor that works out in you and brings forth these glories of identification between you and Christ. It is the Word dwelling in your hearts, richly by faith.

Pray this closing prayer today:

Word of God, indwell me so richly that others might see Thee in me. Amen.

EXCERPTED: "Ye Are Our Epistle," message given at Glad Tidings Tabernacle, 23 August 1922, 2.

The Living Word in You

*In the beginning was the Word,
and the Word was with God, and
the Word was God. The same was
in the beginning with God.
All things were made by him; and
without him was not any thing
made that was made. In him
was life; and the life was
the light of men.*

John 1:1-4

All was made by the Word. I am begotten by His Word. Within me there is a substance that has almighty power in it if I dare believe. Faith going on to be an act, a reality, a deposit of God, an almighty flame moving you to act, so that signs and wonders are manifest. A living faith within an earthen casket.

Are you begotten? Is it an act within you. Some need a touch, a liberty to captives. As many as He touched were made perfectly whole. Faith takes you to the place where God reigns, imbibing God's bountiful store. Unbelief is sin, for Jesus went to death to bring us the light of life.

Prayer Principle #21

God in you is a living substance, a spiritual nature, the living Word. You live by another life, the faith of the Son of God.

As the Holy Ghost reveals Jesus, He is real, the living Word, effective, acting, speaking, thinking, praying, singing in you.

Pray this closing prayer today:

Word of God, birth in me the life of Jesus Christ that He might live fully in me. Amen.

EXCERPTED: "Floodtide," Faith Leaflet No. 2, 3.

Prayer
and Faith

*Therefore I say unto you, What
things soever ye desire, when ye
pray, believe that ye receive them,
and ye shall have them.*

Mark 11:24

While I know prayer is wonderful, and not only changes things, but changes you, while I know the man of prayer can go right in and take the blessing from God, yet I tell you that if we grasp this truth that we have before us, we shall find that faith is the greatest inheritance of all.

May God give us faith that will bring this glorious inheritance to our hearts. Beloved, it is true that the just shall live by faith; and do not forget that it takes a just man to live by faith. May the Lord reveal to us the fullness of this truth that God gave to Abraham.

You cannot find anywhere that God ever failed.

He wants to bring us into that blessed place of faith, changing us into a real substance of faith, till we are so like-minded with Him that whatever we ask, we believe; and believing, we receive; and our joy becomes full because we believe.

Pray this closing prayer today:

As I pray, Lord, fill me with faith, that believing Your Word, I might ask and receive. Amen.

EXCERPTED: "Faith," Faith Booklet No. 1, n.d., 1ff.

The Foundation: God's Word (Part 1)

Therefore whosoever heareth these sayings of mine, and doeth them, I will liken him unto a wise man, which built his house upon a rock: And the rain descended, and the floods came, and the winds blew, and beat upon that house; and it fell not: for it was founded upon a rock.

Matthew 7:24-25

If we are ever going to make any progress in divine life, we shall have to have a real foundation. There is no foundation, only the foundation of faith for us. All our movements, and all that ever will come to us, which is of any importance, will be because we have a *rock*. If you are on the rock, no power can move you. The need of today is the Rock to have our faith firm upon.

Your faith must have something to establish itself on.

Prayer Principle #23

There is not establishment outside of God's Word for you. Everything else is sand. Everything else shall fall.

If you build on anything else but the Word of God — on imaginations, on sentimentality, or any feelings, or any special joy — it will mean nothing to you without a foundation on the Word of God.

Pray this closing prayer today:

Upon the solid rock of Thy Word, I build my life. Jesus, Thou art my Rock; Thou art my foundation. Amen.

EXCERPTED: "Faith (Part One)," message presented at Glad Tidings Tabernacle, 2 August 1922, 2-3.

The Foundation: God's Word (Part 2)

Whosoever cometh to me, and heareth my sayings, and doeth them, I will shew you to whom he is like: He is like a man which built a house, and digged deep, and laid the foundation on a rock: and when the flood arose, the stream beat vehemently upon that house, and could not shake it: for it was founded upon a rock.

Luke 6:47-48

I was going on a tram from London to Blackpool. A man who was a builder stood next to me, and I asked him, "The men are building those houses upon the sands?"

"Oh, you don't know? You're not a builder," he said. "Don't you know that we can pound that sand till it becomes like rock?"

"Nonsense," I said. I saw an argument was not going to profit, so I dropped it. By and by we reached Blackpool where the mountainous waves come over the shore. I saw a row of houses that had fallen flat, and drawing the attention of this builder, I said, "Oh, look at those houses. See how flat they are." He forgot our previous conversation, saying, "You know, here we have very large tides. Those houses built on the sands, when the tides came in, fell flat."

Beloved, it won't do to build on sand.

Prayer Principle #24

We must have something better than sand, and everything is sand except the Word. There isn't anything that will remain.

We are told that heaven and earth will be melted up as a scroll in fervent heat. The Word of God shall last forever. Not one jot or tittle of the Word of God shall fail. If there is anything that is satisfying to me today more than another, it is, "Thy Word is settled in heaven."

Pray this closing prayer today:

Jesus, Your Word is the foundation for all things. Amen.

EXCERPTED: "Faith (Part One)," message presented at Glad Tidings Tabernacle, 2 August 1922, 2-3.

Praying in Harmony

*And when they had prayed, the
place was shaken where they were
assembled together; and they were
all filled with the Holy Ghost, and
they spake the word of God with
boldness. And the multitude of them
that believed were of one heart and
of one soul.*

Acts 4:31-32.

Why could the early church ask in prayer and get anything? One accord, perfect fidelity and love, oneness. God lifts the church in prayer into a place of manifested reconciliation, oneness of accord, until the devil has no power.

Whatsoever things ye desire when ye pray, only believe! I see, beloved, we need to get more love and the Word will do it.

How the Master can move among the needs and perishing when He has the right of way in the church!

Let us be in harmony, in one accord, as we pray with the divine plan having knowledge connected with love. Death to the old having perfect peace in us so that His life power can be manifested.

Pray this closing prayer today:

Lord, teach us to pray together in such unity and in one accord that by faith we might see you do great and mighty things in the church. Amen.

EXCERPTED: "We Mean Business With God," n.p., 4 June 1926, 4-5.

Born of the Word — Incorruptible Seed

*Being born again, not of corruptible
seed, but of incorruptible, by the
word of God, which liveth and
abideth for ever.*

1 Peter 1:23

Y ou are born of an incorruptible power—
the power of God's Word — by his personality and His nature. Ye are begotten of God and are not your own. You are now incarnated. You can believe that you have passed from death unto life and become an heir of God, a joint heir with Christ, in the measure that you believe His Word.

The natural flesh has been changed for a new order. The first order was the natural Adamic order. The last order is Christ — the heavenly order. And now you become changed by a heavenly power existing in an earthly body; a power that can never die: It can never see corruption, and it cannot be lost.

Prayer Principle #26

If you are born of God, you are born of the power of the Word and not of man.

I want you to see that you are born of a power which exists in you, a power of which God took and made the world that you are in.

Pray this closing prayer today:

Thank you, Lord, that I have the privilege to be born of Thy incorruptible seed, Thy Word. Amen.

EXCERPTED: "Filled With God," address given in Melbourne, Australia, n.d., 3-4.

Victory in the Word

O death, where is thy sting? O grave, where is thy victory? The sting of death is sin; and the strength of sin is the law. But thanks be to God, which giveth us the victory through our Lord Jesus Christ.
1 Corinthians 15:55-57

Only Believe! Only Believe! There is a power in God's Word which brings life where death is. To him that believeth this Word, all things are possible.

The Life of the Son is in the Word. Jesus brought life and immortality to our lives through the gospel.

Prayer Principle #27

We can never exhaust the Word.

There is a river, the streams of which make glad the city of God. Jesus Himself has conquered death and given us the victory!

Pray this closing prayer today:

Jesus, Thou art the Word of God that giveth us the victory over sin and death. Amen.

EXCERPTED: "We Mean Business With God," n.p., 4 June 1926, 1.

The Written Word Is Supernatural

All scripture is given by inspiration of God, and is profitable for doctrine, for reproof, for correction, for instruction in righteousness.

2 Timothy 3:16

Here is our attitude of rest: all our hope is in the Word of God. The Word of God abideth forever. Oh, the glorious truths found therein!

Never compare the Book of books with other books. It is from heaven. It doesn't *contain* the Word of God. It *is* the Word of God. Supernatural in origin; eternal in duration and value; unequaled in scope; and divine in authorship is God's Word.

Prayer Principle #28

Read it through. Pray it in. Write it down.

The fear of the Lord is the beginning of wisdom. The knowledge of our weakness brought the greatness of redemption. Knowledge is coupled with joy. You cannot have the knowledge of the Word without joy. Have eternal faith — daring to believe what God has said!

Pray this closing prayer today:

Thank you, Father, for the written Word that reveals Your plan of salvation in Christ Jesus. Amen.

EXCERPTED: "The Moving Breath of the Spirit," n.p., August 1925, 1-2.

The Profit of the Word of God

*For unto us was the gospel
preached, as well as unto them: but
the word preached did not profit
them, not being mixed with faith in
them that heard it.*

Hebrews 4:2

The Word quickens the preacher, the hearer and everybody. The Word giveth life, and God wants it to be so alive in you that you will be moved as it is preached. Oh, it is lovely to think that God can change you in a moment and can heal you in a moment. When God begins, who can hinder?

Sometimes a thing comes before me, and I realize that nothing but the Word of God can do it. I meet all classes of people — people who have no faith — and I find the Word of God quickens them, even those who have no knowledge of salvation. The gospel of the

Lord Jesus Christ does cure everything.

My dear ones, it is impossible for God to fail you. If you hear the Word of God, it will stimulate you to know as sure as you live that God will bring you out of this condition.

Prayer Principle #29

It is impossible to know the Word of God without knowing that He will meet you.

Pray this closing prayer today:

Oh, Word of God, quicken me, stimulate me, heal me, save me in Jesus' mighty name. Amen.

EXCERPTED: "Ordination," address given in Adelaide, Australia, n.d., 2-3.

The Holy Spirit Prays in Us

*And, behold, the Lord passed by,
and a great and strong wind rent
the mountains, and brake in pieces
the rocks before the Lord; but the
Lord was not in the wind: and after
the wind an earthquake; but the
Lord was not in the earthquake:
And after the earthquake a fire; but
the Lord was not in the fire: and
after the fire a still small voice.*

1 Kings 19:11-12

How do you come to God? Where is God? Is He in the air? In the wind? He that cometh to God, where is He? God is in you. Oh, hallelujah! And you will find the Spirit of the Living God in you, which is the prayer circle; which is the lifting power; which is the revelation element; which is the divine power that lifts you.

He that cometh to God is already in the place where the Holy Ghost takes the prayers and swings them out according to the mind of the Spirit. For who hath known the mind of Christ, or who is able to make intercession but the mind of the Spirit of the Living God. Where is He? He is in us!

Prayer Principle #30

Oh, the baptism of the Holy Ghost is an inward presence of the personality of God, which lifts, prays, takes hold and lives in tranquility of peace and power that rests and says, "It is all right."

God answers prayers because the Holy Ghost prays; your advocate is Jesus; and the Father is the judge of all. There He is. Is it possible for any prayer to miss on those lines?

Pray this closing prayer today:

Spirit of God, pray in me, through me and in spite of me. Amen.

EXCERPTED: "Faith (Part Two)," message presented at Glad Tidings Tabernacle, 3 August 1922, 6.

The Wigglesworth Series

The following thirty-day devotionals
are also available.

Smith Wigglesworth on Healing

Smith Wigglesworth believed that every
believer could be baptized in the Holy
Spirit and that God could perform miracles
today as He did in the early church. Grasp
these truths as you use this devotional to
inspire and encourage your own faith.

Smith Wigglesworth on Faith

Smith Wigglesworth often challenged his
listeners by saying, "Faith is an act. Faith is
a leap. Faith jumps in. Faith claims. Faith's
author is Jesus." Let his perspective on
faith challenge you as you read this thirty-
day devotional.

Available at your local Christian
bookstore or from:

Creation House
600 Rinehart Road
Lake Mary, FL 32746
1-800-283-8494